SCHOLASTIC

Revision Mini-Lessons

Grade 3

By Sarah Glasscock

NEW YORK · TORONTO · LONDON · AUCKLAND · SYDNEY
MEXICO CITY · NEW DELHI · HONG KONG · BUENOS AIRES

Teaching *Resources*

Cover Design by Jaime Lucero

Interior Design by Sydney Wright

Interior Illustrations by Kelly Kennedy

ISBN-13: 978-0-439-70487-8
ISBN-10: 0-439-70487-1
Copyright © 2006 by Sarah Glasscock
All rights reserved.
Printed in the U.S.A.

1 2 3 4 5 6 7 8 9 10   40   13 12 11 10 09 08 07 06

CONTENTS

INTRODUCTION

One of the most difficult things about writing is making sure that we have successfully translated the ideas in our head to the words on the page. The goal in writing is to communicate effectively so that the reader is transported and not disappointed or confused. Revising is an essential part of the writing process. By going over what we've written, we show ownership of and pride in our words.

How to Use This Book

This book includes lessons on seven topics: subject-verb agreement, nouns and pronouns, verbs, word choice (including adjectives and adverbs), main idea and details, purpose and audience, and punctuation and spelling. Students often experience difficulties with one or more of these topics in their writing. While some become adept at catching errors as they work, others write without ever looking back at what they've written. Yet every writer benefits from taking the time to revise a piece of writing.

Each lesson contains two thematically linked passages with errors for students to revise. One passage is nonfiction, and the other is fiction. To serve as a reference for students, a cartoon and a reminder about a key aspect of the topic appear above each passage. The first error in each passage is corrected on the page. I suggest that you read aloud the passage as students follow along. By using the rhythm of your voice and intonation, you'll be able to highlight the errors in a passage, for example, making your delivery flat as you read a series of repeated nouns or stumbling over misspelled words.

The corresponding teaching page contains a bulleted list of common errors associated with the topic, a review section called Replay, troubleshooting tips, and a section with suggestions about how to present the passage and model the correction shown. These are only suggestions—feel free to tailor the lesson to the needs of your students and your teaching style.

After you and your students have discussed the passage, it's their turn to become editors. A checklist appears at the bottom of this page as a guide. Before students copy their revision on the blank reproducible page, have them write it out on a separate sheet of paper. This will give them some leeway in revising more before they actually publish their final draft.

Sample revisions appear in an answer key at the back of the book, along with a list of proofreader's marks and a writing checklist. Make sure students are familiar with and comfortable using the proofreader's marks before they tackle the passages.

Encourage your students to make these passages their own. Although the focus of a passage may be on subject-verb agreement, they should make any other changes they feel would strengthen the passage.

I hope this book helps your students—and you—feel that revision can be a pleasure.

We Work Together: SUBJECTS AND VERBS

A sentence has to have a subject and a verb—and the two must agree with each other in number.

Your students may encounter the following problems with subjects and verbs in their writing:

- Leaving out the subject or the verb. Do they know who or what is committing the action in a sentence?
- Selecting the wrong form of the verb to go with the subject. Do they pair singular nouns with plural verbs?

Replay

List three subjects and three verbs on the board. Include a proper noun, irregular forms of verbs, and singular and plural forms. Use the list below, or create your own.

Subjects	Verbs
sheep	flies
Sinbad	float
balloons	sleep

Ask students to match the subjects and verbs that can go together—for example, *sheep/sleep, Sinbad/flies, balloons/float.* Talk about why some nouns and verbs, such as *balloons/flies,* don't go together (*balloons,* a plural noun requires a plural verb form, but *flies* is singular). Also point out that each verb in the list matches the noun *sheep* because sheep can be either singular or plural. To wrap up the review, have students select a subject and a verb from the list and use them in a sentence.

Troubleshoot

Share these tips with your class.

- ✓ Some students may have trouble identifying the subject and verb of a sentence. Remind them that subjects are nouns or pronouns. The subject tells who or what does the action in the sentence. The verb describes that action. Point out that putting the subject and verb together will always create a simple sentence: *Tom studies.*
- ✓ Reading, reading, and more reading can help students develop an ear for irregular subjects and verbs. Take the opportunity to point out irregular forms as you read aloud.

- ✓ Remind students that the subject in an imperative sentence may not be stated directly. In an imperative sentence such as, *Please be quiet,* the subject *you* is understood.
- ✓ The subject and the verb may not always appear next to each other. A phrase may separate them. This sentence appears in the second paragraph of "Hoops and More Hoops": *People in Greece swung hoops to lose weight.*

Model

"Hoops and More Hoops": Explain that you will be reading a passage that tells about how people have played with hoops over the years. Ask students to follow along on their copies as you read aloud. Talk about students' responses to the passage and any experiences they have had playing with hoops. Then remind them that the passage contains some errors. Go over the first error on the page. You might say the following: *I see an error in the very first sentence. The subject of the sentence is "Children." "Children" is a plural noun. That means there is more than one child. "Enjoys" is a singular verb. The verb should be plural to match the noun. The subject and verb should be "Children enjoy." The sentence should read: "Children enjoy playing with hoops."* As students go over the passage on their own, circulate around the room to answer any questions and to spot any problems. Note that the passage contains several verb tenses.

"Toy Joy": This passage is a fantasy written in the present tense. Briefly discuss the genre with students. Then read aloud the passage as students follow along on their own copies. After discussing the content, turn to the error shown on the page. You may model it like this: *The second sentence has an error. The subject of this sentence is " walls and floors." Both "walls" and "floors" are plural. The verb is "is covered," which is singular. Remember that the verb agrees with the subject, not the noun that is closest to it. The phrase "of his tree-house room" is between the subject and verb. But "room" is not the subject of the sentence. The sentence should read: "The walls and floors of his tree-house room are covered with toys."*

We Work Together: **Subjects and Verbs**

Read the passage below.

Remember: A sentence must have a subject and a verb.

Going to the store.

You are going to the store. Is that what you mean?

Hoops and More Hoops

Children enjoys playing with hoops. You can roll hoops. You can throw hoops. You can swing them around different parts of your body.

Long ago in Egypt, kids rolled hoops made out of grape vines. They used sticks to roll the hoops along the ground. Also swung the hoops around the middle of their bodies. People in Greece swung hoops to lose weight. Later, in England, both kids and adults played with hoops. In the 1950s, Australian children used bamboo hoops in gym class. They swung the hoops around their waists.

Two Americans heard about the Australian hoops. They thought hoops would make great toys. They tested their plastic hoops on playgrounds. Real kids swung these hoops around their middles—and loved it! The hoops was called hula hoops. Dancers from Hawaii do the hula dance. Their hips move back and forth. When you're spinning a hula hoop, you have to move your hips to keep the plastic hoops from clattering to the ground.

Soon, millions of hula hoops were sold. Hula hoop contests was held all over the country. One woman spun 82 of them—at the same time!

Who know? Maybe your grandkids will be playing with hoops, too.

Does each sentence have a subject and a verb?
Do all the subjects and verbs agree with each other?
Is the writing as clear and exciting as it could be?
Reread the passage. Then, mark any changes you want to make. The first change has been made for you.

Revision Mini-Lessons • Grade 3 • Scholastic Teaching Resources

We Work Together: **Subjects and Verbs**

Read the checklist at the bottom of the page. Then, go over your revision to "Hoops and More Hoops" again. Copy it on the lines below.

_____

_____

_____

_____

_____

_____

_____

_____

_____

_____

_____

_____

_____

_____

_____

_____

_____

_____

_____

_____

_____

_____

Checklist

❑ Does each sentence have a subject and a verb?

❑ Do all the subjects and verbs agree with each other?

❑ Is the writing as clear and exciting as it could be?

We Work Together: **Subjects and Verbs**

Read the passage below.

Remember: The subject and verb in a sentence must agree with each other.

Toy Joy

are
∧
Barton James loves toys more than anything. The walls and floors of his tree-house room is covered with toys. He plays with all of them. That doesn't leave much time for Barton to do his chores. He is supposed to oil Daisy, the robot dog, every morning. Usually, Barton forget. He is too busy playing with his toys.

Finally, Barton's mother has had it. "There will be no more time travel for you, Barton James. You is staying right here in the year 2100. You have to learn to do your chores."

Barton can't believe it. Wants to go back to the year 1958 so he can buy a hula hoop. In 1958 a hula hoop costs less than a dollar. Barton can't buy one hula hoop now. It would cost him over five hundred dollars! He don't have that much money.

Then Barton has an idea. He stays up all night working on his plan. Soon, the floor of his room is covered with computer chips, wires, and pieces of toys. Barton tests his plan the next morning. He turns on his toy fire engine. "Find Daisy. Feed her," he says. The engine rolls away. It stops in front of Daisy. The tiny firefighters points a hose at Daisy. Oil flows into Daisy's open mouth.

That weekend, Barton and his mom travels back to 1958. They come back with two hula hoops—one for each of them.

Does each sentence have a subject and a verb?
Do all the subjects and verbs agree with each other?
Is the writing as clear and exciting as it could be?
Reread the passage. Then, mark any changes you want to make.
The first change has been made for you.

We Work Together: **Subjects and Verbs**

Read the checklist at the bottom of the page. Then, go over
your revision of "Toy Joy" again. Copy it on the lines below.

_____

_____

_____

_____

_____

_____

_____

_____

_____

_____

_____

_____

_____

_____

_____

_____

_____

_____

_____

_____

_____

_____

Checklist

❏ Does each sentence have a subject and a verb?

❏ Do all the subjects and verbs agree with each other?

❏ Is the writing as clear and exciting as it could be?

Revision Mini-Lessons • Grade 3 • Scholastic Teaching Resources

She and I: NOUNS AND PRONOUNS

Passages "Eileen Collins: Reaching for Her Dream" (nonfiction)
"Lighting Up the Sky" (fiction)

Curriculum Area Science

Using pronouns appropriately ensures that repetition doesn't weaken a passage.

Your students may encounter the following problems in replacing nouns with pronouns in their writing:

- Using the incorrect pronoun. Do students replace a singular noun with a plural pronoun?
- Being unclear about whom or what the pronoun refers to. Does the reader know that *she* refers to Lucy and not to Mrs. Hamilton?
- Neglecting to balance the use of nouns and pronouns. Do students alternate nouns and pronouns?

Replay

Select a boy and a girl to come to the front of the room. Tell the class: *She wrote a poem.* Ask the class to identify which student you're talking about. Call on volunteers to explain how they identified the correct student. Next select two girls to come to the front of the class. Repeat the sentence, and ask students whether they can identify the correct student now. Challenge them to revise your sentence by substituting another pronoun—for example: *They wrote a poem.* Then review subjective and objective pronouns as necessary with a chart like the one below.

Subjective Case (subjects)	Objective Case (objects)
I ran out of the woods.	Those horns scared **me**.
You should have seen that moose!	That moose would have scared **you**, too.
It was big, brown, and shaggy.	All the neighbors spotted **it**.
She saw the moose through the window.	Jason told **her** to call the police.
He didn't believe a moose was outside.	I told **him** to call the police.
We shouted at the moose.	Four police officers saved **us**.
You should have seen the moose's antlers.	They want **you** to describe the moose.
They must have been two feet long!	Tell **them** that it was big, brown, and shaggy!

Troubleshoot

Share these tips with your class.

✓ Some contractions are formed using pronouns and verbs—*I'm, I've, he'll, she'd, it's, they're,* and so on. Emphasize the importance of the apostrophe: It takes the place of the letter(s) that are dropped. Remind students that *it's* is the contraction for *it is* and that *its* is a possessive pronoun.

✓ Students often have trouble understanding that nouns such as *class, group,* and *family* are singular and should be replaced with the pronoun *it* rather than *they.* Use these nouns as the subjects of sentences. Then have students identify the singular verbs you paired with these nouns.

Model

"Eileen Collins: Reaching for Her Dream": Tell students that you will be reading aloud a short biography of astronaut Eileen Collins. Ask if anyone has heard of Commander Collins. Pass out the passage and have students follow along as you read. Then discuss Eileen Collins's story with the class. Model your response to the first error shown on the page: *I see an error in the second sentence of the passage. The writer used the pronoun "her" as the subject of the sentence. The pronoun "she" is always used as the subject of a sentence. I can make sure that "she" should be the subject. I can identify the verb, which is "didn't know." Then I can ask myself: Who or what didn't know? The answer is "she" (Eileen Collins).*

"Lighting Up the Sky": Hand out the passage, and explain that it is a fictional story about a girl who sees the space shuttle that Eileen Collins commanded. Read aloud the passage as students follow along. Point out the first error on the page by saying something like this: *I know the main character is Leela. Her name is repeated too many times in the third sentence. Since the second sentence also contains her name, I would use pronouns in the third sentence. Let me read aloud the two sentences with the change: "Leela couldn't sleep. She tossed and turned so much that Leela almost fell out of bed." I would make another change to the sentence. I'd write it this way: "She tossed and turned so much that she almost fell out of bed."* Read aloud the first three sentences with the changes so students can hear the new rhythm of the revised sentences.

She and I: **Nouns and Pronouns**

Read the passage below.

Remember: Use the correct pronoun. *She* can be a subject, but *her* never is.

Her likes sunflower seeds.

She likes sunflower seeds. I like them, too.

Eileen Collins: Reaching for Her Dream

She
^
Growing up, astronaut Eileen Collins always knew she wanted to fly. ~~Her~~ just didn't know how far she'd fly! Eileen grew up in Elmira, New York. Planes often flew over her home. These planes didn't have engines. It were called gliders. They flew by gliding on the air. Eileen would watch the planes in the deep blue sky and dream.

Eileen first thought about becoming an astronaut in the fourth grade. She'd always enjoyed math and science in school. The idea of learning more about space was exciting to her.

At 19, Eileen took her first plane ride. It was also Eileen Collins's first flying lesson. Eileen worked for three years to save enough money for the lessons. Luckily, Eileen learned that Eileen really loved to fly!

In 1978, the National Aeronautics and Space Administration (NASA) let women join its space shuttle program. That year, Eileen was training to become a pilot with the Air Force. Her kept working hard. In 1990, NASA asked she to be an astronaut!

So far, Eileen has flown over 6,000 hours. More than 500 of those hours were in space. She was the first woman to fly the space shuttle. She was also the first woman to lead a team into space.

What does Eileen Collins think about her dream now? "I think it's been a lot of hard work and a little bit of luck to get here, but I'm happy I'm here. I don't think I could have a better job."

Are the correct pronouns taking the place of nouns?

Does the passage contain a good mix of nouns and pronouns?

Is the writing as clear and exciting as it could be?

Reread the passage. Then, mark any changes you want to make. The first change has been made for you.

Revision Mini-Lessons • Grade 3 • Scholastic Teaching Resources

She and I: **Nouns and Pronouns**

Read the checklist at the bottom of the page. Then, go over your revision of "Eileen Collins: Reaching for Her Dream" again. Copy it on the lines below.

_____

_____

_____

_____

_____

_____

_____

_____

_____

_____

_____

_____

_____

_____

_____

_____

_____

_____

Checklist

❑ Are the correct pronouns taking the place of nouns?

❑ Does the passage contain a good mix of nouns and pronouns?

❑ Is the writing as clear and exciting as it could be?

❑ Reread the passage. Then mark any changes you would make. The first change has been made for you.

She and I: **Nouns and Pronouns**

Read the passage below.

Remember: A pronoun can take the place of a noun in a sentence.

Lighting Up the Sky

She
^

Tomorrow was the big math test. Leela couldn't sleep. She tossed and turned so much that ~~Leela~~ almost fell out of bed. Her teacher, Mr. Rushdie, had worked with her on division. Her mother had made flash cards for her. Her older brother had explained long division over and over. Her father had said, "I think math is hard, too."

There must be something wrong with my brain, Leela thought. I love learning about history and important events. I can rattle off important dates. Why can't I use mental math to figure out what 720 divided by 90 is? Is it 8 or 80? Maybe it's 9 or 90. Leela pulled the covers over her head. Leela swallowed. Leela's throat felt a little dry and scratchy. I can't go to school tomorrow if I'm sick, Leela thought. Leela smiled and drifted off to sleep.

"Wake up! Leela, wake up!" Leela's father shook her bed. "Hurry, or you'll miss it!"

"I'm sick. I can't go to school. I can't take the test," Leela answered sleepily. Why was it still dark?

Her father scooped her out of bed, covers and all. He carried her into the backyard. Leela's mother and brother were staring up at the sky.

"What is going on?" Leela asked.

"There it is!" Her brother pointed at a streak of light in the sky.

Leela caught Leela's breath. The light kept traveling. The light left a trail of smoke.

"The space shuttle is on its way to Florida," her mother explained. "This is the first time a woman's landed it."

"We just saw history being made," her brother said.

"Eileen Collins is flying the shuttle," Leela's father said. "Eileen Collins used to be a math teacher. You know what Eileen Collins said? She said, 'I know a lot of students struggle with math, but if you work hard enough, you're going to get it.'"

Leela traced the trail of smoke that was still in the sky. She wanted to fly across the sky, too. "I'd better work harder at math, then," Leela sighed.

"We'll help," her family said.

Are the correct pronouns taking the place of nouns?

Does the passage contain a good mix of nouns and pronouns?

Is the writing as clear and exciting as it could be?

Reread the passage. Then mark any changes you would make. The first change has been made for you.

14

She and I: **Nouns and Pronouns**

Read the checklist at the bottom of the page. Then, go over your revision of "Lighting Up the Sky" again. Copy it on the lines below.

_____

_____

_____

_____

_____

_____

_____

_____

_____

_____

_____

_____

_____

_____

_____

_____

_____

_____

_____

_____

Checklist

❑ Are the correct pronouns taking the place of nouns?

❑ Does the passage contain a good mix of nouns and pronouns?

❑ Is it clear who or what each pronoun refers to?

15

Eat or Gulp?: VERBS

Passages "Lighthouse Day" (nonfiction)
"Saved!" (fiction)

Curriculum Area Social Studies

Verbs are the engines of sentences.

Your students may encounter the following problems with verbs in their writing:

- Using the wrong tense. Do they use the present tense with the time marker *yesterday*?

- Choosing an incorrect form of an irregular verb. Do students write *goed* instead of *went*?

- Repeating the same verbs. Do they overuse *to be* verbs?

Replay

Go over the simple verb tenses with students, and include examples of both regular and irregular verbs such as *jump*, *fly*, and *to be*. You may want to use a chart like the one below.

Past (Yesterday)	Present (Today)	Future (Tomorrow)
I jumped.	I jump.	I will jump.
You jumped.	You jump.	You will jump.
He jumped.	She jumps.	It will jump.
We jumped.	We jump.	We will jump.
They jumped.	They jump.	They will jump.

Guide students in expanding these sentences or creating new ones that contain these verbs. Then write the following sentence on the board: *The snake left.* Challenge students to supply more active and vivid verbs to describe the snake's departure. Pose questions such as the following to fire their imaginations: "Was the snake in a hurry, or was it taking its time? How did the snake move? Did it seem surprised or lazy or scared?"

Troubleshoot

Share these tips with your class.

✓ Remind students that compound verbs must share the same tense. You may also want to review subject and verb agreement, which is discussed on page 6.

✓ Review some common contractions and their verb tenses: *I'd* (past: I had), *I'm* (present: I am), *I've* (present: I have), *I'll* (future: I will).

✓ Students often repeat the same verbs in their writing. Start a set of synonym envelopes for your class. On the front of the envelopes, write the commonly overused verbs you see in your classroom. When you encounter a more exact or exciting synonym for one of those verbs during read-aloud time or independent reading, write the verb and the sentence it appears in on an index card and place it in the appropriate envelope. Encourage students to browse through these envelopes to increase their verb vocabulary.

Model

"Lighthouse Day": The errors in this nonfiction passage are related to verb tenses. Read aloud the passage as students follow along. Discuss the content, and ask if anyone has ever visited or seen a lighthouse. Then explain the correction shown on the page: *The first sentence uses the word "visit." "Visit" is a present-tense verb. But I see the time words "Last summer." Those words tell me that the verb should be in the past tense. The sentence should read: "Last summer, my family and I visited a lighthouse."* Before students tackle the passage on their own, remind them to look for time words to give them clues about which verb tense to use.

"Saved!": Explain that this fictional passage is based on a real event that happened over a hundred years ago at the Egg Island lighthouse. The students' task is to replace some of the verbs with more vivid ones. Ask them to follow along as you read aloud the passage. After talking about the events in the story, introduce the first correction. You may want to say something like this: *The verb "went" is the correct verb tense. The story took place in the past. However, the writer could have used a stronger verb. Think about what Milo the dog did. He and Fred Taylor were playing a game of fetch. Fred tossed the stick into the water. What did the dog do? Imagine a dog going after a stick in the water. He would jump. He might also leap or hop.* Before students begin their revisions, have them take a few minutes to imagine the events in the story. Encourage them to be bold in their verb substitutions.

Eat or Gulp?: **Verbs**

Read the passage below.

Remember: Verbs have three tenses: present, past, and future. Look for words that tell which verb tense to use.

It rains last night.

Last night, it *rained*.

Lighthouse Day

Last summer, on August 7, my family and I visit^ed a lighthouse. Do you want to know why? August 7 is National Lighthouse Day. We always go to a lighthouse on that day. Lighthouses are important. They kept boats from running into dangerous rocks. They guide ships safely to land.

Do you know when the first lighthouse was built in this country? The Boston Light is built in 1716. (*Light* means the same as *lighthouse*.) It stands near the city of Boston. Fog is a problem for boats and ships. Long ago, the keeper of the Boston Light used to shoot a cannon. In the fog, the loud boom warned ships away from the rocks.

Last summer, we saw the Boston Light. A lighthouse keeper still lives there today. This person turns on the light at night. Then he or she turned off the light in the morning. The Boston Light is the only American lighthouse with a keeper. All the other lighthouses are run by machines. The Boston Light is the oldest lighthouse in this country. So it will always have a keeper. One day, I am the keeper of the Boston Light.

Do the verb tenses match the time words?
Do each subject and verb agree?
Is the writing as clear and exciting as it could be?
Reread the passage. Then, mark any changes you want to make.
The first change has been made for you.

17

Eat or Gulp?: **Verbs**

Read the checklist at the bottom of the page. Then, go over your revision of "Lighthouse Day" again. Copy it on the lines below.

_____

_____
_____
_____
_____
_____
_____
_____
_____
_____
_____
_____
_____
_____
_____
_____
_____
_____
_____

Checklist

❏ Do the verbs match the time words?
❏ Are the verbs as exciting as they could be?
❏ Do each subject and verb agree?

Revision Mini-Lessons • Grade 3 • Scholastic Teaching Resources

Eat or Gulp?: **Verbs**

Read the passage below.

Remember: Use exciting verbs in your writing.

Saved!

Fred Taylor waved as the boat left Egg Island. Most of the time, the Taylors were alone on the island—until summer. Then lots of people rowed out to the island. They wanted to see the lighthouse.

Fred tossed a stick into the sea. Milo immediately ∧ ~~went~~ **jumped** into the water. He made a huge splash. Milo was a very large dog. He swam against the waves. The stick moved farther away from the island. Milo swam faster. He snatched the stick in his mouth. Soon, Milo was back on Egg Island. He dropped the stick at Fred's feet. Then Milo shook himself dry. Fred got wet again.

Two chickens pecked the ground nearby. A goat walked among the rocks. Milo didn't pay any attention to them. He didn't even look up at the Egg Island lighthouse. He sat, wagged his tail, and waited for Fred to throw the stick again.

It was getting dark. Soon, Fred's father would turn on the light in the Egg Island lighthouse. Fred clapped his hands. "Time to go home, Milo!"

Fred went toward the stone house. It was connected to the lighthouse. He lived there with his parents and his four brothers and sisters.

Suddenly, Fred heard Milo barking. The dog went past Fred. He ran toward the other end of Egg Island.

"Dad!" Fred said. "Somebody's in trouble!" He went after Milo.

A boat was in the waves. The people on board shouted and pointed at the water. Fred saw a dark spot in the ocean. Milo went toward it. Then the dog began to come back to the island. He was dragging a girl by the collar of her dress.

Fred's dad went into the water. He lifted the girl. She coughed. The people on the boat cheered.

Fred hugged Milo. "You've done it again! Good boy!"

Milo wagged his tail.

Do the verb tenses match the time words?
Do each subject and verb agree?
Is the writing as clear and exciting as it could be?
Reread the passage. Then, mark any changes you would make.
The first change has been made for you.

Eat or Gulp?: **Verbs**

> Read the checklist at the bottom of the page. Then, go over your revision of "Saved!" again. Copy it on the lines below.

_____

_____

_____

_____

_____

_____

_____

_____

_____

_____

_____

_____

_____

_____

_____

_____

_____

_____

_____

_____

Checklist

❏ Do the verbs match the time words?

❏ Are the verbs as exciting as they could be?

❏ Do each subject and verb agree?

The ~~Quiet~~ Silent Rooster: WORD CHOICE

Passages	"The World's Largest Buffalo" (nonfiction) "Dear Dan" (fiction)

Curriculum Area	Math

Using vivid language, including adjectives and adverbs, makes writing come alive.

Your students may encounter the following problems with word choice in their writing:

- Including too many adjectives and adverbs, or not using enough.
- Repeating the same words.
- Using vague language, or language that doesn't sound natural.

Replay

Review the role of adjectives and adverbs with a chart such as the one below.

	ADJECTIVES	ADVERBS
What They Modify	Nouns	Verbs, Adjectives, Adverbs
Questions They Answer	What kind? The *silent* rooster pecked. How many? *Several* roosters crowed. Which ones? *That* rooster looks mean.	How? The roosters ate *quickly*. Where? The rooster scurried *outside*. When or How Often? The roosters ran away *today*. The roosters run away *often*.

When students make conscious decisions about which words to use, they are developing their own writing voices. Incorporating sensory language into their writing can help them discover how unique their voice is. Bring in a variety of objects, such as sandpaper, a small gong or bell, a piece of ripe fruit, a flower, and graham crackers. Allow small groups of students to use their senses to really study each object. Then ask them to write as many words as they can to describe the object. Emphasize that they should not censor themselves; instead, they should write down the associations that flood into their minds as they touch, taste, feel, see, or smell the objects. (NOTE: Make sure students understand that they are also making choices about which senses to apply to each object; for example, they wouldn't taste the bell or the flower. Monitor groups closely as they work.)

Troubleshoot

Share these tips with your class.

✓ As students experiment with words, their writing can become flowery. They may begin to lose the naturalness of their voice. So students can really hear what they've written, encourage them to read their work aloud. Model this by pointing out the rhythm in a piece you've written, and how certain words slow or stop the flow. Also, use examples of your work that contain places where your voice falters or changes. Work individually with students to help them strengthen their listening skills as they write.

✓ Have a thesaurus available for students to consult as they work. Point out that successful word choice is not simply about substituting one word for another. The writer has to make a choice based on the type of writing he or she is creating, whether the word will enhance his or her voice, and how the word plays with the rest of the sentence. Above all, use the thesaurus to cultivate a love for words in your students.

Model

"The World's Largest Buffalo": Before passing out the passage, reveal the title. Tell students that the passage is nonfiction, and ask them what they think it will be about. Then read aloud the passage as students follow along. After discussing whether their predictions were correct, model your response to the correction on the page. You might say something like this: *I agree with the change. I would delete the word "large," too. The sentence already tells me exactly how large the buffalo is: it's 26 feet tall. That's very large. And, as I read the passage, I noticed that the word "large" is used a lot in the first paragraph. What other words can you think of that mean the same as "large?"* Although this passage focuses on the repetition of certain words, encourage students to replace any words that they feel could be more precise and descriptive.

"Dear Dan": As you pass out this passage, explain that it's a piece of fiction in the form of a letter. The main character is writing about seeing the World's Largest Buffalo. Read aloud the passage as students follow along. Talk about the content and what students think of the voice. Does the writer sound natural? Segue into a discussion of the correction on the page: *I know that sometimes people exaggerate when they write letters or tell a story about something they've seen. But using the adjectives "interesting," "amazing," and "unusual" to talk about the clues didn't sound real to me. Using only one of those adjectives would have sounded more natural. And, as I read aloud the clues, I was thinking that they were very unusual. I would have said either "unusual clues" or "amazing clues."*

The ~~Quiet~~ Silent Rooster: **Word Choice**

Read the passage below.

Remember: Make every word count. Try not to use the same words over and over again

You are a pretty bird. Your beak is pretty. Your feathers are pretty.

I am a very handsome parrot. My shiny yellow beak curves. My feathers are as green as leaves.

The World's Largest Buffalo

The land around Jamestown, North Dakota, is flat. Visitors can easily spot the ~~large~~ 26-foot-tall buffalo in town. Many stop to have their pictures taken in front of the large buffalo. Back home, who's going to believe they actually saw the world's largest buffalo? From head to tail, the buffalo is 46 feet long. It's 14 feet wide. That's a large buffalo!

Herds of buffalo once lived near Jamestown. But many buffalo were killed all across the United States in the 1800s. Jamestown built the large statue to honor these beautiful animals. Today, visitors can see a live herd of buffalo near the statue. (And they're not 26 feet tall, either!)

Jamestown also has the oldest grocery store in North Dakota. The grocery store was built in 1878 in another town. Later, the grocery story was moved to Jamestown. (No, the world's largest buffalo didn't help move the grocery store!) People can buy sodas, postcards, and other gifts at the grocery store.

Visit Jamestown, North Dakota. Be sure to have your picture taken in front of the world's largest buffalo. Your friends will be amazed! (And don't forget to have your photo taken in front of the live buffalo, too!)

Can you picture what the writer is describing?
Are some words used too many times?
Is the writing as clear and exciting as it could be?
Reread the passage. Then mark any changes you would make.
The first change has been made for you.

Revision Mini-Lessons • Grade 3 • Scholastic Teaching Resources

The ~~Quiet~~ Silent Rooster: **Word Choice**

Read the checklist at the bottom of the page. Then, go over your revision of "The World's Largest Buffalo" again. Copy it on the lines below.

_____

_____

_____

_____

_____

_____

_____

_____

_____

_____

_____

_____

_____

_____

_____

_____

_____

_____

Checklist

❑ Do the words paint clear pictures in your mind?

❑ Are some words used too many times?

❑ Would you change any nouns or verbs?

❑ Would you add any adjectives or adverbs?

The ~~Quiet~~ Silent Rooster: **Word Choice**

Read the passage below.

Remember: Using too many adjectives or adverbs won't make your writing clear.

Your green, shiny, beautiful, amazing, pretty feathers shine.

My beautiful green feathers do shine.

Dear Dan

July 8, 2006

Dear Dan,

    Guess what I saw today! I'll give you some ~~interesting,~~ amazing, ~~unusual~~ clues. It's the biggest one in the world. It weighs 60 tons. That's 120,000 pounds! (I told you it was huge.) It's the color of mud. It has four small, little, tiny legs and sharp horns with sharp points. Do you give up? Today, I saw the World's Largest Buffalo! Don't worry—it's not a real animal. Someone made the buffalo out of concrete.

    Guess how much it cost to make the big, large, huge, giant beast. It cost $11,000. Guess when the buffalo was made. It was built in the 1950s. We weren't even born yet. Guess where the World's Largest Buffalo lives. Jamestown, North Dakota, is its home. Guess how many people stop to see the buffalo each year. More than 100,000 people stop. Now, that number includes my family and me.

    Guess what Spots thought of the giant buffalo. The hair rose on the back of her neck. She snarled and growled and howled and yelped. She ran up to the big large huge giant beast and barked at its small, little, tiny, right leg. Then Spots turned around and hid behind me.

    Guess where we're going next summer. We're driving all the way to Odessa, Texas. The World's Largest Jackrabbit lives there. Maybe you can come with us!

See you soon,
Missy

Can you picture what the writer is describing?

Are some words used too many times?

Is the writing as clear and exciting as it could be?

Reread the passage. Then mark any changes you would make. The first change has been made for you.

The ~~Quiet~~ Silent Rooster: **Word Choice**

Read the checklist at the bottom of the page. Then, go over your revision of "Dear Dan" again. Copy it on the lines below.

_____

_____

_____

_____

_____

_____

_____

_____

_____

_____

_____

_____

_____

_____

_____

_____

_____

_____

_____

_____

_____

Checklist ·

❏ Do the words paint clear pictures in your mind?

❏ Are some words used too many times?

❏ Would you change any nouns or verbs?

❏ Would you add any adjectives or adverbs?

What's It All About?: MAIN IDEA AND DETAILS

A main idea is like a trail. Details are the signs that make sure no one gets lost.

Your students may encounter the following problems with main idea and details in their writing:

- Failing to state a main idea.
- Neglecting to include enough details to support the main idea.
- Adding unrelated and unnecessary details.

Replay

Tell students that a main idea is exactly what it sounds like: It's the big idea or the main focus of a paragraph or an essay. It reveals what the paragraph or essay is about. Details give more information about the main idea. They support it. Remind students that a writer states the main idea at or near the beginning of a piece of work, but it's not necessarily always the first sentence. Then go over the main idea and details below. Challenge students to identify which detail(s) are unnecessary because they don't support the main idea.

Main Idea: All third graders should learn how to multiply.

Detail: People often have to multiply when they shop.

Detail: Three times six is eighteen. *(unnecessary)*

Detail: They may not always have a calculator.

Create a short paragraph on an overhead or on the board. Think out loud as you model how to phrase the main idea and to include relevant details. Slip in one or two unnecessary details. Ask students to help you revise your paragraph.

Troubleshoot

Share these tips with your class.

✓ Use sentence strips to help students determine whether a detail is related to the main idea. Isolate the main-idea strip, and then have students place a detail strip below it. Ask them if the detail sentence really supports the main idea.

✓ It can be easy for students to lose the connection to a main idea as they write. They may turn a supporting detail into another main idea and use details to support it instead of the true main idea. Although the supporting details must be related, each one has to serve the main idea. If students

wander from their topics, ask them to plug their main ideas and details into a web to make sure that each detail really supports the main idea.

Model

"Explaining Earthquakes": This passage is missing a main idea. A correction is not shown on the page so you and your students can work together to create one. Distribute the passage, and then read it aloud as students follow along. Begin a discussion of the content by asking: *What is this passage all about? How do you know?* Guide students as necessary in inferring what the main idea is from the clues that the details give. Then have students think of a main idea. You might guide them in this way: *We agreed that this passage is about the stories people used to make up to explain earthquakes. The title "Explaining Earthquakes" also gives us a clue about what the main idea should be. How should we state the main idea in a sentence?* Help students craft and shape a main idea. Assure them that they can refine the main idea when they work independently on the passage. Also caution students to watch out for unnecessary details in the passage.

"When the Cow Tosses Her Head": This is a retelling of an East African folktale. It contains several unnecessary details. After reading aloud the passage to students, discuss the folktale. Ask students if they could picture the earth, cow, stone, and fish. Then model your response to the correction shown on the page: *I would have deleted the last sentence in the first paragraph, too. Do you see how it makes the story swerve off course? The storyteller says she is going to tell us about what the world looks like. Explaining that she catches fish in a pond doesn't tell us anything about what the world looks like. She had been talking about fish, but it was a giant fish, not a little fish in a pond. In this story, the giant fish helping to hold up the world and little fish in a pond don't have anything in common. Listen as I read aloud the paragraph without that sentence.* Ask students whether the main idea of the paragraph of the story was affected by the removal of the sentence. Suggest they use this strategy to determine whether a detail is necessary: Read the paragraph without the sentence. Does the meaning of the paragraph change? Is it as strong as it was before?

26

What's It All About?: **Main Idea and Details**

Read the passage below.

Remember: A main idea tells what a piece of writing is about. Details support the main idea.

I read a book about how to teach a parrot to talk. I didn't understand it.

Was the main idea missing?

Explaining Earthquakes

Today, we know why earthquakes happen. Energy builds up in the earth. The earth moves suddenly to let that energy go. ∧

People in Mongolia thought that a frog caused earthquakes. They believed that a huge frog carried the earth on its back. Whenever the frog moved, the earth moved, too.

In India, people told a story about animals holding up the earth, too. They said that elephants held up the earth. The elephants stood on top of a turtle in its shell. The turtle was on top of a snake. When any of the animals moved, the earth shook and quaked. My aunt lives in India.

Siberia is a very cold place. Its earthquake story had dogs, sleds—and fleas! The earth sat on a sled. A team of dogs pulled the sled. But the dogs had fleas. They must not have had flea collars. Each time they scratched, the earth trembled.

A West African folktale said that the earth was flat. A giant and a mountain held it up. The giant's wife made sure the sky didn't fall down. Sometimes, the giant couldn't stop himself. He had to hug his wife. That made the earth shake. There really aren't any giants.

A giant was also the star of another West African folktale. The earth rested on this giant's head. All the plants in the world were his hair. Animals and people were like bugs crawling through the giant's hair. Usually, the giant sat quietly. But sometimes, he turned to the west. Then, he turned back to the east. What happened then? Earthquake!

Suppose you lived thousands of years ago. How do you think you would have explained earthquakes?

Is the main idea clearly stated?

What details are included?

Is the writing as clear and exciting as it could be?

Reread the passage. Then mark any changes you would make.

Revision Mini-Lessons • Grade 3 • Scholastic Teaching Resources

What's It All About?: **Main Idea and Details**

Read the checklist at the bottom of the page. Then, go over your revision of "Explaining Earthquakes" again. Copy it on the lines below.

_____

_____

_____

_____

_____

_____

_____

_____

_____

_____

_____

_____

_____

_____

_____

_____

_____

_____

_____

_____

_____

_____

_____

_____

Checklist

❑ Is the main idea clearly stated?

❑ Do all the details support the main idea?

❑ Are all the details important?

What's It All About?: **Main Idea and Details**

Read the passage below.

Remember: The main idea tells what a piece of writing is about. Details support the main idea.

I'm going to clean your cage. Seeds have spilled on the floor. Your mirror is dirty. I have to clean the kitchen.

I thought you were going to clean my cage.

When the Cow Tosses Her Head

A Folktale From East Africa

Listen, and I will tell you what the world looks like. The earth spins on one horn of a huge cow. The cow stands, very carefully, on top of a stone. The stone rests on the back of a giant fish. Think of it like this: earth, cow, stone, fish. I catch little fish in the pond near here.

You might think that the earth would quake if the fish moved. No, the fish was always calm. The fish was a catfish. He didn't mind the weight of the stone and the cow and the earth. Of course, the fish was resting on a bed of soft sand. The weight of the stone and the cow and the earth didn't bother the fish's back.

Every once in a while, the fish felt a tiny shiver when the cow moved her hooves. "Be careful," the fish would warn the cow. The cow was white with brown patches. "You know what will happen if you move too much!"

The cow did know what would happen. But the earth was very heavy. It was difficult to stand on the stone. Often, the weight of the world made the cow's neck hurt. Cow would stand the pain as long as she could. Then, she'd toss her head. She had soft, brown eyes. The earth would fly from one horn to the other. The seas would rock. Large waves would sweep across the shore. Cracks would split the earth. Trees and houses would fall down.

At the very bottom, on her soft bed of sand, the fish felt the trembling of the earth. "Cow! What have you done!"

The cow was always sorry about the trouble she caused on the earth. "I'll never, ever toss my head again," she'd promise. But sooner or later, her neck would begin to hurt again. My neck would hurt, too. Cow would toss her head and stretch her neck. The earth would fly to her other horn. And you know what would happen then—earthquake!

Is the main idea clearly stated?

Do all the details belong with the main idea?

Is the writing as clear and exciting as it could be?

Reread the passage. Then, mark any changes you would make. The first change has been made for you.

Name _____ Date _____

What's It All About?: **Main Idea and Details**

Read the checklist at the bottom of the page. Then, go over your revision of "When the Cow Tosses Her Head" again. Copy it on the lines below.

Checklist

❑ Is the main idea clearly stated?
❑ Do all the details support the main idea?
❑ Are all the details important?

Revision Mini-Lessons • Grade 3 • Scholastic Teaching Resources

That Was So Funny: PURPOSE AND AUDIENCE

Passages	"You're Invited!" (nonfiction) "When Is the Party?" (fiction)	**Curriculum Area**	Language Arts

You wouldn't expect to see the competitors at a swim meet wearing red clown noses. The purpose of the swimmers isn't to make the audience laugh—although the swimmers probably wouldn't mind hearing some cheering and clapping.

Your students may encounter the following problems with purpose and audience in their writing:

- Difficulty identifying the purpose of and audience for a particular piece.
- Straying from their original purpose.
- Using the wrong tone to convey their purpose to readers.

Replay

Display a book you've recently shared with students, and ask them to summarize it. Begin a discussion of purpose and audience with the following questions: *Why do you think the author wrote this book? What do you think his or her purpose was? Who do you think the author wants to read this book? Who is his or her audience?* When students respond, determine what kinds of clues they used to identify the purpose and audience. Review the purpose and audience for several other fiction and nonfiction books your students are familiar with.

Troubleshoot

Use these tips with your class.

✓ Students often use an overly formal voice in expository writing. Emphasize that their writing voices should remain natural and distinctive, no matter what genre they're writing in. Their voice must engage the reader as much as, if not more than, the facts they present.

✓ A writer's passion for a topic is at the heart of good writing. If a student feels that he or she has nothing to say about a topic, try to discover any personal connection to the material that the student has.

✓ Remind students to read aloud their work as they write. This practice can help them hear the rhythm of their writing and the naturalness (or awkwardness) of their voice. Their audience will appreciate the effort.

Model

"You're Invited!": Before handing out this passage and reading it aloud, ask students what the purpose of an invitation is. Talk about the essential details that an invitation must have. Then read aloud the invitation, and go over the correction shown on the page: *We know that the party is not being held at Luis and Summer's house. The invitation clearly states that the party is going to be at Blue Hills City Park. The address of Luis and Summer's house should be deleted. People may become confused. They may show up there instead of the park. The writer forgot the purpose of the invitation. One of its purposes is to make sure people know where to go.* You may want to go over the invitation line by line with students, and then let them rewrite it independently.

"When Is the Party?": Read aloud the passage as students follow along. If you're teaching this lesson in sequence, tie the story back to the invitation that students revised. Begin your discussion of the content by modeling your response to the correction shown on the page: *I like the change that was made here. It's important to let your readers know what kind of story it is and who it's about. After reading the story, I know that it's not a mystery. In this type of story, a writer shouldn't keep readers guessing. That might confuse them. They might start making predictions about the story that aren't correct. They may feel disappointed that the story didn't turn out the way they thought it would. Remember: It's the writer's job to lead readers through a story.* Remind students to identify the purpose of the story and keep it in mind as they work on their revision.

You may want to work with students to help them decipher the vocabulary in the first sentence of the third paragraph.

31

That Was So Funny: **Purpose and Audience**

Read the passage below.

Remember: Be clear about your purpose for writing. Is it to present facts? Is it to make your reader laugh?

You're Invited!

You're invited to a birthday party for Luis and Summer Holden!

Date: October 29, 2006

Time: 1pm to 4pm

Where: Blue Hills City Park

How to Get There:

~~Luis and Summer live at 302 Sunshine Circle.~~

Go south on Main Street. You'll pass my favorite toy store. It's on the right.

Turn left at Fourth Street.

Go six blocks. You'll pass Blue Hills School. It's on the left. That's where I go to school. Mrs. Cruz is my teacher. I really like her.

Turn right at Dripping Springs Road. I've never seen any springs beside this road.

Go two miles. You'll drive over the river. My grandparents like to fish in the river.

Take the first right after the river. That's Blue Hills City Park.

Follow the signs to the pond. Park anywhere in the lot. But I'd park in the shade if I were you.

We'll have blue and green balloons tied to the trees, so you can't miss us!

Hope you can come!

Can you tell why the author wrote this passage?

Who does he or she want to read this piece?

Is the writing as clear as it could be?

Reread the passage. Then, mark any changes you would make. The first change has been made for you.

Revision Mini-Lessons • Grade 3 • Scholastic Teaching Resources

That Was So Funny: **Purpose and Audience**

Read the checklist at the bottom of the page. Then, go over your revision of "You're Invited!" again. Copy it on the lines below.

_____

_____

_____

_____

_____

_____

_____

_____

_____

_____

_____

_____

_____

_____

_____

_____

_____

_____

Checklist

❑ Is the purpose of the passage clear?
   Does the writer want to inform or entertain the reader?

❑ Who is the audience?
   Who is the writer hoping to reach?

33

That Was So Funny: **Purpose and Audience**

Read the passage below.

Remember: Think about who your readers are. Will they be able to understand what you're writing?

Say the word *flabbergasted.*

I don't know what *flabbergasted* means.

When Is the Party?

It was noon. The pond in Blue Hill City Park was quiet. Except for the Holdens' car, the parking lot was empty. It shouldn't have been. **Luis and Summer Holden's birthday party was supposed to start at noon.**

Luis batted a green balloon. "Where is everybody?" he asked.

Summer surveyed the perimeters of the park. She didn't see anyone she knew. "Maybe they're hiding," she said. "Maybe they're throwing us a surprise party."

Several picnic tables were spread with paper tablecloths. A bowl of fruit sat on each table. Smoke was rising from the barbecue pit. Mr. Holden poked the coals with a long fork. "The fire's almost ready! We can put on the hamburgers soon!" The hamburger was probably invented in Germany.

Mrs. Holden put the last paper plate on the table. "We should probably wait until someone gets here," she said. Mrs. Holden's birthday was November 4.

Summer kept checking her new birthday watch. Soon it was 12:15. In New York, it was 1:15. In California, it was 10:15. The United States has different time zones. "Nobody's coming to our party," she wailed.

"But Eric and Taylor promised they were coming!" Luis said. "Everybody said they were coming!"

Mrs. Holden's cell phone rang. "Hello?" She listened for a few seconds. Then she smiled. "No, come early. We're already here at the park."

She hung up. "That was Eric's dad. He thinks the party starts at one o'clock."

Summer looked at Luis. "Did you proofread the invitations?"

Luis shook his head. "I thought you did."

They quickly read over an invitation. The time was wrong, but the date and place and directions were right. By one o'clock, the park was filled with Luis and Summer's friends.

Can you tell why the author wrote this passage?

Who does he or she want to read this piece?

Is the writing as clear and exciting as it could be?

Reread the passage. Then, mark any changes you would make. The first change has been made for you.

That Was So Funny: **Purpose and Audience**

Read the checklist at the bottom of the page. Then, go over your revision of "When Is the Party?" again. Copy it on the lines below.

_____

_____

_____

_____

_____

_____

_____

_____

_____

_____

_____

_____

_____

_____

_____

_____

_____

_____

Checklist ·

☐ Is the purpose of the passage clear?

  Does the writer want to inform or entertain the reader?

☐ Who is the audience?

  Who is the writer hoping to reach?

See or Sea?: PUNCTUATION AND SPELLING

A piece of writing without proper punctuation and spelling will confuse and frustrate readers.

Your students may encounter the following problems with punctuation and spelling in their writing:

- Failing to capitalize the first word in a sentence or proper nouns.
- Omitting end punctuation, or using incorrect punctuation.
- Confusing homonyms.

Replay

Punctuation: Write a series of sentences that don't have capitals or punctuation on the board or overhead. Be sure to include a variety of declarative, interrogatory, and exclamatory sentences. Here's a sampling:

1. my brother's name is sam
2. have you ever been to washington, d.c.
3. raise your hand before you speak
4. dr. glass works at the hospital
5. how far is the museum from here

Call on volunteers to rewrite the sentences correctly, and to talk about the clues they used to make the corrections. Be sure to point out that the second sentence is a question. The period at the end goes with the abbreviation *D.C.* To extend the review, prepare a short paragraph that describes your classroom—without using any capital letters or punctuation. Ask students to help you correct it. As you work together, question students about how they decided when one sentence ended and the next one began.

Spelling: Review some common homonyms with students. Explain that some English words sound the same but have different meanings and, usually, different spellings, such as *see/sea, there/their/they're, to/two/too, here/hear*, and so on.

Troubleshoot

Share these tips with your class.

✓ One of the best ways for students to strengthen their spelling skills is by reading, reading, reading. Exposure to properly spelled words, in context, can help reinforce young readers' spelling skills.

✓ Punctuating dialogue or direct quotations is often difficult for students. When you encounter dialogue in a story, take the time to discuss its form. Point out how speech is set off from the rest of the text by a comma and quotation marks. When you spot a direct quotation in nonfiction, tell students that quotation marks are used to set off someone's exact words. The quotation marks guarantee that the person's words are quoted accurately.

Model

"The Red-Bellied Snake": Read aloud this nonfiction passage as students follow along. You may want to emphasize the errors in punctuation and spelling by emphasizing your confusion and hesitancy as you read. Talk about how the errors made you stumble somewhat as you read. Think aloud about the correction shown on the page: *The marks mean that "the" should begin with a capital "T." The word starts a new sentence, and we know that all sentences must begin with a capital letter.* Students may ask why *red-bellied snake* is not a proper noun. Explain that there are different kinds of red-bellied snakes, such as the Northern red belly and the Eastern red belly snakes. Only the proper adjectives are capitalized. You may also point out that other snakes, such as garter snakes and rattlesnakes, are not capitalized, either.

"A Safe Hiding Place": Again, as you read aloud this story, use your voice to show how punctuation and spelling errors can confuse readers. Then ask students what they thought of the story. Which character did they identify with the most—Billy and his concerns, his mother and her dislike of snakes, or his snake-loving grandmother? Turn students' attention to the correction shown on the page. You might explain it like this: *The word "they're" is a contraction for "they are." The sentence "They are was no sign of Mr. Redbelly!" doesn't make sense. That sentence has two verbs—"are" and "was"—and the verbs are different tenses. The subject also doesn't make sense. The writer meant to use the word "there." The words "there," "their," and "they're" sound alike, but they're spelled differently—and they have very different meanings.* Point out that students may have to "undo" a contraction to make sure they've used it correctly in a sentence.

See or Sea?: **Punctuation and Spelling**

Read the passage below.

Remember: A sentence always begins with a capital letter. Proper nouns do, too.

The Red-Bellied Snake

The red-bellied snake really does have a bright red belly. the rest of the snake may be black, gray, or brown. Stripes also run down its back. There may be four dark stripes, or there may be one light stripe. Three pale spots also dot this snake's neck

These snakes love to hide under rocks, leaves, logs, and boards. The area around old barns and houses is one of their favorite places. sometimes, they move into empty aunthills or the burrows of other animals. red-bellied snakes like to eat insects, earthworms, and tiny frogs.

If a red-bellied snake is scared, it won't bite. It might curl up its top lip to show its fear. It might also give off a strong smel. A red-bellied snake might even play dead. It uses these tricks to get people and other animals to leave it alone.

Young snakes are born in July or august. A mother snake might give birth to as many as 21 baby snakes at one time The babys are about three inches long. Grown snakes are usually ate to ten inches long.

Do the sentences begin with capital letters?
Do they end with periods, question marks, or exclamation points?
Are any words spelled wrong?
Is the writing as clear and exciting as it could be?
Reread the passage. Then, mark any changes you would make.
The first change has been made for you.

Revision Mini-Lessons • Grade 3 • Scholastic Teaching Resources

See or Sea?: **Punctuation and Spelling**

Read the checklist at the bottom of the page. Then, go over your revision of "The Red-Bellied Snake" again. Copy it on the lines below.

_____

_____
_____
_____
_____
_____
_____
_____
_____
_____
_____
_____
_____
_____
_____
_____
_____
_____
_____
_____
_____

Checklist ·

❏ Does each sentence begin with a capital letter?
❏ Is each sentence punctuated correctly?
❏ Are any words misspelled?

Revision Mini-Lessons • Grade 3 • Scholastic Teaching Resources

See or Sea?: **Punctuation and Spelling**

Read the passage below.

Remember: Some words sound alike, such as see and sea. But they have different meanings and different spellings.

Do you see the sea?

I see the sea through the window.

A Safe Hiding Place

There

Billy stared into the glass tank. He couldn't believe it. The tank was empty! ~~They're~~ was no sign of Mr. Redbelly! Billy looked under his bed. He saw a baseball bat, a green sock, and a puzzle. There was no snake under the bed.

"What are you looking for, Billy?" his mother aksed.

billy bumped his head on the bed. "Ouch! Nothing!" His mother didn't like snakes at all. He had had to beg and plead to buy Mr. Redbelly. He had had to promise that the snake would never, ever get loose

"Well, come on down. Dinner's redy," she said. "Your grandmother's made your favorite—meatballs!

Mr. redbelly wasn't stretched out on the stairs. He wasn't curled up in a corner of the kitchen. Billy peeked under the table. All he saw were three pairs of feet.

"What are you loking for, Billy?" his mother asked

his grandmother patted him on the back. "Eat your food before it gets cold."

Billy swallowed a bite. It felt like he had a whole meatball stuck in his throat. "It's good," he said. he looked under the table again—just in case.

His mother jumped out of her chair. "You're not looking for that snak, are you!"

Billy took another bite so he wouldn't have to answer her. then his grandmother patted his knee. Mr. Redbelly's head was poking out of her apron pocket. She looked at Billy and winked.

"Sit down, Mela. Eat your food before it gets cold," Billy's grandmother sad

"Don't worry, Mom," Billy said. "Mr. Redbelly's right where he belongs."

Do the sentences begin with capital letters?

Do they end with periods, question marks, or exclamation points?

Are any words spelled wrong?

Is the writing as clear and exciting as it could be?

Reread the passage. Then, mark any changes you would make.

The first change has been made for you.

Revision Mini-Lessons • Grade 3 • Scholastic Teaching Resources

See or Sea?: **Punctuation and Spelling**

Read the checklist at the bottom of the page. Then, go over your revision of "A Safe Hiding Place" again. Copy it on the lines below.

_____

_____

_____

_____

_____

_____

_____

_____

_____

_____

_____

_____

_____

_____

_____

_____

_____

_____

_____

_____

_____

_____

Checklist ·

❑ Does each sentence begin with a capital letter?

❑ Is each sentence punctuated correctly?

❑ Are any words misspelled?

Revision Mini-Lessons • Grade 3 • Scholastic Teaching Resources

Answer Key Sample revisions are given.

Subjects and Verbs, p. 7

Hoops and More Hoops

Children enjoy playing with hoops. You can roll hoops. You can throw hoops. You can swing them around different parts of your body.

Long ago in Egypt, kids rolled hoops made out of grape vines. They used sticks to roll the hoops along the ground. They also swung the hoops around the middle of their bodies. People in Greece swung hoops to lose weight. Later, in England, both kids and adults played with hoops. In the 1950s, Australian children used bamboo hoops in gym class. They swung the hoops around their waists.

Two Americans heard about the Australian hoops. They thought hoops would make great toys. They tested their plastic hoops on playgrounds. Real kids swung these hoops around their middles—and loved it! The hoops were called hula hoops. Dancers from Hawaii do the hula dance. Their hips move back and forth. When you're spinning a hula hoop, you have to move your hips to keep the plastic hoops from clattering to the ground.

Soon, millions of hula hoops were sold. Hula hoop contests were held all over the country. One woman spun 82 of them—at the same time!

Who knows? Maybe your grandkids will be playing with hoops, too.

Subjects and Verbs, p. 9

Toy Joy

Barton James loves toys more than anything. The walls and floors of his tree-house room are covered with toys. He plays with all of them. That doesn't leave much time for Barton to do his chores. He is supposed to oil Daisy, the robot dog, every morning. Usually, Barton forgets. He is too busy playing with his toys.

Finally, Barton's mother has had it. "There will be no more time travel for you, Barton James. You're staying right here in the year 2100. You have to learn to do your chores."

Barton can't believe it. He wants to go back to the year 1958 so he can buy a hula hoop. In 1958 a hula hoop costs less than a dollar. Barton can't buy one now. It would cost him over five hundred dollars! He doesn't have that much money.

Then Barton has an idea. He stays up all night working on his plan. Soon, the floor of his room is covered with computer chips, wires, and pieces of toys. Barton tests his plan the next morning. He turns on his toy fire engine. "Find Daisy. Feed her." The engine rolls away. It stops in front of Daisy. The tiny firefighters point a hose at Daisy. Oil flows into Daisy's open mouth.

That weekend, Barton and his mom travel back to 1958. They come back with two hula hoops—one for each of them.

Nouns and Pronouns, p. 12

Eileen Collins: Reaching for Her Dream

Growing up, astronaut Eileen Collins always knew she wanted to fly. She just didn't know how far she'd fly! Eileen grew up in Elmira, New York. Planes often flew over her home. These planes didn't have engines. They were called gliders. They flew by gliding on the air. Eileen would watch the planes in the deep blue sky and dream.

Eileen Collins first thought about becoming an astronaut in the fourth grade. She'd always enjoyed math and science in school. The idea of learning more about space was exciting to her.

At 19, Eileen took her first plane ride. It was also her first flying lesson. She worked for three years to save enough money for the lessons. Luckily, Eileen learned that she really loved to fly!

In 1978, the National Aeronautics and Space Administration (NASA) let women join its space shuttle program. That year, Eileen was training to become a pilot with the Air Force. She kept working hard. In 1990, NASA asked her to be an astronaut!

So far, Eileen has flown over 6,000 hours. More than 500 of those hours were in space. She was the first woman to fly the space shuttle. She was also the first woman to lead a team into space.

What does Eileen Collins think about her dream now? "I think it's been a lot of hard work and a little bit of luck to get here, but I'm happy I'm here. I don't think I could have a better job."

Nouns and Pronouns, p. 14

Lighting Up the Sky

Tomorrow was the big math test. Leela couldn't sleep. She tossed and turned so much that she almost fell out of bed. Her teacher, Mr. Rushdie, had worked with her on division. Her mother had made flash cards for her. Her older brother had explained long division over and over. Her father had said, "I think math is hard, too."

There must be something wrong with my brain, Leela thought. I love learning about history and important events. I can rattle off important dates. Why can't I use mental math to figure out what 720 divided by 90 is? Is it 8 or 80? Maybe it's 9 or 90. Leela pulled the covers over her head. She swallowed. Her throat felt a little dry and scratchy. I can't go to school tomorrow if I'm sick, she thought. She smiled and drifted off to sleep.

"Wake up! Leela, wake up!" Her father shook her bed. "Hurry, or you'll miss it!"

"I'm sick. I can't go to school. I can't take the test," Leela answered sleepily. Why was it still dark?

Her father scooped her out of bed, covers and all. He carried her into the backyard. Her mother and brother were staring up at the sky.

"What is going on?" Leela asked.

"There it is!" Her brother pointed at a streak of light in the sky.

Leela caught her breath. The light kept traveling. It left a trail of smoke.

"The space shuttle is on its way to Florida," her mother explained. "This is the first time a woman's landed it."

"We just saw history being made," her brother said.

"Eileen Collins is flying the shuttle," Leela's father said. "She used to be a math teacher. You know what she said? She said, 'I know a lot of students struggle with math, but if you work hard enough, you're going to get it.'"

Leela traced the trail of smoke that was still in the sky. She wanted to fly across the sky, too. "I'd better work harder at math, then," she sighed.

"We'll help," her family said.

Verbs, p. 17

Lighthouse Day

Last summer, on August 7, my family and I visited a lighthouse. Do you want to know why? August 7 is National Lighthouse Day. We always go to a lighthouse on that day. Lighthouses are important. They keep boats from running into dangerous rocks. They guide people to land safely.

Do you know when the first lighthouse was built in this country? The Boston Light was built in 1716. (*Light* means the same as *lighthouse*.) It stands near the city of Boston. Fog is a problem for boats and ships. Long ago, the keeper of the Boston Light used to shoot a cannon. In the fog, the loud boom warned ships away from the rocks.

Last summer, we saw the Boston Light. A lighthouse keeper still lives there today. This person turns on the light at night. Then he or she turns off the light in the morning. The Boston Light is the only American lighthouse with a keeper. All the other lighthouses are run by machines. The Boston Light is the oldest lighthouse in this country. So it will always have a keeper. One day, I will be the keeper of the Boston Light.

Answers (*Continued*)

Verbs, p. 19

Saved!

Fred Taylor waved as the boat left Egg Island. Most of the time the Taylors were alone on the island—until summer. Then lots of people rowed out to the island. They wanted to see the lighthouse.

Fred tossed a stick into the sea. Milo immediately jumped into the water. He made a huge splash. Milo was a very large dog. He paddled against the waves. The stick floated farther away from the island. Milo paddled faster. He snatched the stick in his mouth. Soon, Milo was back on Egg Island. He dropped the stick at Fred's feet. Then Milo shook himself dry. Fred got wet again.

Two chickens pecked the ground nearby. A goat wandered among the rocks. Milo didn't pay any attention to them. He didn't even look up at the Egg Island lighthouse. He sat, wagged his tail, and waited for Fred to throw the stick again.

It was getting dark. Soon, Fred's father would turn on the light in the Egg Island lighthouse. Fred clapped his hands. "Time to go home, Milo!"

Fred ran toward the stone house. It was connected to the lighthouse. He lived there with his parents and his four brothers and sisters.

Suddenly, Fred heard Milo barking. The dog bounded past Fred. He ran toward the other end of Egg Island. "Dad!" Fred called. "Somebody's in trouble!" He followed Milo.

A boat rocked in the waves. The people on board shouted and pointed at the water. Fred saw a dark spot in the ocean. Milo swam toward it. Then the dog began to swim back to the island. He was dragging a girl by the collar of her dress.

Fred's dad ran into the water. He lifted the girl. She coughed. The people on the boat cheered.

Fred hugged Milo. "You've done it again! Good boy!"

Milo wagged his tail.

Word Choice, p. 22

The World's Largest Buffalo

The land around Jamestown, North Dakota, is flat. Visitors can easily spot the 26-foot-tall buffalo in town. Many stop to have their pictures taken in front of the huge animal. Back home, who's going to believe they actually saw the world's largest buffalo? From head to tail, the buffalo is 46 feet long. It's 14 feet wide. That's a big buffalo!

Herds of buffalo once lived near Jamestown. But many buffalo were killed all across the United States in the 1800s. The town built the giant statue to honor these beautiful animals. Today, visitors can see a live herd of buffalo near the statue. (And they're not 26 feet tall, either!)

Jamestown also has the oldest grocery store in North Dakota. The store was built in 1878 in a nearby town. Later, it was moved to Jamestown. (No, the world's largest buffalo didn't help move it!) People can buy sodas, postcards, and other gifts at the store.

Visit Jamestown, North Dakota. Be sure to have your picture snapped in front of the world's largest buffalo. Your friends will be amazed! (And don't forget to have your photo taken in front of the live buffalo, too!)

Answers *(Continued)*

Word Choice, p. 24

Dear Dan

July 8, 2006

Dear Dan,

   Guess what I saw today! I'll give you some amazing clues. It's the biggest one in the world. It weighs 60 tons. That's 120,000 pounds! (I told you it was huge.) It's the color of mud. It has four tiny legs and sharp horns. Do you give up? Today, I saw the World's Largest Buffalo! Don't worry—it's not a real animal. Someone made the buffalo out of concrete.

   Guess how much it cost to make the big beast. It cost $11,000. Guess when the buffalo was made. This happened in the 1950s. We weren't even born yet. Guess where the World's Largest Buffalo lives. Jamestown, North Dakota, is its home. Guess how many people stop to see the buffalo each year. More than 100,000 people stop. Now that number includes my family and me.

   Guess what Spots thought of the giant buffalo. The hair rose on the back of her neck. She snarled and growled. She ran up to the big beast and barked at its right leg. Then she turned around and hid behind me.

   Guess where we're going next summer. We're driving all the way to Odessa, Texas. The World's Largest Jackrabbit lives there. Maybe you can come with us!

See you soon,

Missy

Main Idea and Details, p. 27

Explaining Earthquakes

   Today, we know why earthquakes happen. Energy builds up in the earth. The earth moves suddenly to let that energy go. Long ago, people made up stories to explain earthquakes. Almost every part of the world has a folktale about what causes an earthquake.

   People in Mongolia thought that a frog caused earthquakes. They believed that a huge frog carried the earth on its back. Whenever the frog moved, the earth moved, too.

   In India, people told a story about animals holding up the earth, too. They said that elephants held up the earth. The elephants stood on top of a turtle in its shell. The turtle was on top of a snake. When any of the animals moved, the earth shook and quaked.

   Siberia is a very cold place. Its earthquake story had dogs, sleds—and fleas. The earth sat on a sled. A team of dogs pulled the sled. But the dogs had fleas. Each time they scratched, the earth trembled.

   A West African folktale said that the earth was flat. A giant and a mountain held it up. The giant's wife made sure the sky didn't fall down. Sometimes, the giant couldn't stop himself. He had to hug his wife. That made the earth shake.

   A giant was also the star of another West African folktale. The earth rested on this giant's head. All the plants in the world were his hair. Animals and people were like bugs crawling through the giant's hair. Usually, the giant sat quietly. But sometimes, he turned to the west. Then, he turned back to the east. What happened then? Earthquake!

   Suppose you lived thousands of years ago. How do you think you would have explained earthquakes?

Main Idea and Details, p. 29

When the Cow Tosses Her Head:

A Folktale From East Africa

Listen, and I will tell you what the world looks like. The earth spins on one horn of a huge cow. The cow stands, very carefully, on top of a stone. The stone rests on the back of a giant fish. Think of it like this: earth, cow, stone, fish.

You might think that the earth would quake if the fish moved. No, the fish was always calm. He didn't mind the weight of the stone and the cow and the earth. Of course, the fish was resting on a bed of soft sand. The weight of the stone and the cow and the earth didn't bother the fish's back.

Every once in a while, the fish felt a tiny shiver when the cow moved her hooves. "Be careful," the fish would warn the cow. "You know what will happen if you move too much!"

The cow did know what would happen. But the earth was very heavy. It was difficult to stand on the stone. Often, the weight of the world made the cow's neck hurt. Cow would stand the pain as long as she could. Then, she'd toss her head. The earth would fly from one horn to the other. The seas would rock. Large waves would sweep across the shore. Cracks would split the earth. Trees and houses would fall down.

At the very bottom, on her soft bed of sand, the fish felt the trembling of the earth. "Cow! What have you done!"

The cow was always sorry about the trouble she caused on the earth. "I'll never, ever toss my head again," she'd promise. But sooner or later, her neck would begin to hurt again. Cow would toss her head and stretch her neck. The earth would fly to her other horn. And you know what would happen then—earthquake!

Purpose and Audience, p. 32

You're Invited!

You're invited to a birthday party for Luis and Summer Holden!

Date: October 29, 2006

Time: 1pm to 4pm

Where: Blue Hills City Park

How to Get There:

Go south on Main Street. You'll pass a toy store. It's on the right.

Turn left at Fourth Street.

Go six blocks. You'll pass Blue Hills School. It's on the left.

Turn right at Dripping Springs Road.

Go two miles. You'll drive over the river.

Take the first right after the river. That's Blue Hills City Park.

Follow the signs to the pond. Park anywhere in the lot.

We'll have blue and green balloons tied to the trees, so you can't miss us!

Hope you can come!

Answers (*Continued*)

Purpose and Audience, p. 34

When Is the Party?

It was noon. The pond in Blue Hill City Park was quiet. Except for the Holdens' car, the parking lot was empty. It shouldn't have been. Luis and Summer Holden's birthday party was supposed to start at noon.

Luis batted a green balloon. "Where is everybody?" he asked.

Summer looked around the park. "Maybe they're hiding. Maybe they're throwing us a surprise party."

Several picnic tables were spread with paper tablecloths. A bowl of fruit sat on each one. Smoke was rising from the barbecue pit. Mr. Holden poked the coals with a long fork. "The fire's almost ready! We can put on the hamburgers soon!"

Mrs. Holden put the last paper plate on the table. "We should probably wait until someone gets here," she said.

Summer kept checking her new birthday watch. Soon it was 12:15. "Nobody's coming to our party," she wailed.

"But Eric and Taylor promised they were coming!" Luis said. "Everybody said they were coming!"

Mrs. Holden's cell phone rang. "Hello?" She listened for a few seconds. Then she smiled. "No, come early. We're already here at the park."

She hung up. "That was Eric's dad. He thinks the party starts at one o'clock."

Summer looked at Luis. "Did you proofread the invitations?"

Luis shook his head. "I thought you did."

They quickly read over an invitation. They sighed. At least the date and place and directions were right. By one o'clock, the park was filled with their friends.

Punctuation and Spelling, p. 37

The Red-Bellied Snake

The red-bellied snake really does have a bright red belly. The rest of the snake may be black, gray, or brown. Stripes also run down its back. There may be four dark stripes, or there may be one light stripe. Three pale spots also dot this snake's neck.

These snakes love to hide under rocks, leaves, logs, and boards. The area around old barns and houses is one of their favorite places. Sometimes, they move into empty anthills or the burrows of other animals. Red-bellied snakes like to eat insects, earthworms, and tiny frogs.

If a red-bellied snake is scared, it won't bite. It might curl up its top lip to show its fear. It might also give off a strong smell. A red-bellied snake might even play dead. It uses these tricks to get people and other animals to leave it alone.

Young snakes are born in July or August. A mother snake might give birth to as many as 21 baby snakes at one time. The babies are about three inches long. Grown snakes are usually eight to ten inches long.

Punctuation and Spelling, p. 39

A Safe Hiding Place

Billy stared into the glass tank. He couldn't believe it. The tank was empty! There was no sign of Mr. Redbelly! Billy looked under his bed. He saw a baseball bat, a green sock, and a puzzle. There was no snake under the bed.

"What are you looking for, Billy?" his mother asked.

Billy bumped his head on the bed. "Ouch! Nothing!" His mother didn't like snakes at all. He had had to beg and plead to buy Mr. Redbelly. He had had to promise that the snake would never, ever get loose.

"Well, come on down. Dinner's ready," she said. "Your grandmother's made your favorite—meatballs!"

Mr. Redbelly wasn't stretched out on the stairs. He wasn't curled up in a corner of the kitchen. Billy peeked under the table. All he saw were three pairs of feet.

"What are you looking for, Billy?" his mother asked.

His grandmother patted him on the back. "Eat your food before it gets cold."

Billy swallowed a bite. It felt like he had a whole meatball stuck in his throat. "It's good," he said. He looked under the table again—just in case.

His mother jumped out of her chair. "You're not looking for that snake, are you!"

Billy took another bite so he wouldn't have to answer her. Then his grandmother patted his knee. Mr. Redbelly's head was poking out of her apron pocket. She looked at Billy and winked.

"Sit down, Mela. Eat your food before it gets cold," Billy's grandmother said.

"Don't worry, Mom," Billy said. "Mr. Redbelly's right where he belongs."

Proofreader's Marks

Symbol	Meaning	Example
∧	Add a word or phrase	**lonely** The ∧ puppy sighed. **in his sleep** The puppy sighed∧.
ℽ	Delete a letter or a word	The dark chocolate brown puppy yappℽed. The ~~deep, dark~~ chocolate brown puppy yapped.
≡	Capitalize	The active puppies at pet world tumbled in their pen. ≡ ≡
/	Lowercase	My D̸ad brought home a Border Collie puppy.
∿	Transpose letters	Border collies are one of the smartest breeds of dogs.
⊙ ? !	Change end punctuation	**?** Do you have any pets∧ **⊙** I have two dogs and three hamsters?
¶	Begin a new paragraph	¶My dog, Buster, loves to jump on the couch. He enjoys watching TV with me.

Writing Checklist

Subjects and Verbs

❑ Does each sentence have a subject and a verb?

❑ Do all the subjects and verbs agree with each other?

Nouns and Pronouns

❑ Are the correct pronouns taking the place of nouns?

❑ Does the passage contain a good mix of nouns and pronouns?

❑ Is it clear who or what each pronoun refers to?

Verbs

❑ Do the verbs match the time words?

❑ Are the verbs as exciting as they could be?

❑ Do each subject and verb agree?

Word Choice

❑ Do the words paint clear pictures in your mind?

❑ Are some words used too many times?

❑ Would you change any nouns or verbs?

❑ Would you add any adjectives or adverbs?

Main Idea and Details

❑ Is the main idea clearly stated?

❑ Do all the details support the main idea?

❑ Are all the details important?

Purpose and Audience

❑ Is the purpose of the passage clear? Does the writer want to inform or entertain the reader?

❑ Who is the audience? Who is the writer hoping to reach?

Punctuation and Spelling

❑ Does each sentence begin with a capital letter?

❑ Is each sentence punctuated correctly?

❑ Are any words misspelled?